Practice Management Compendium

Part 2: Organising the Practice

Practice Management Compendium

Part 1: Understanding the Contract
Part 2: Organising the Practice
Part 3: Finance and Reports
Part 4: Clinical Practices

Practice Management Compendium

Part 2: Organising the Practice

by

John Fry

and

Kenneth Scott
General Practitioners

and

Pauline Jeffree
Practice Nurse,
Beckenham, Kent

KLUWER ACADEMIC PUBLISHERS
DORDRECHT / BOSTON / LONDON

Distributors

for the United States and Canada : Kluwer Academic Publishers, P.O. Box 358, Accord Station, Hingham, MA 02018-0358, U.S.A.

for all other countries : Kluwer Academic Publishers Group, Distribution Center, P.O. Box 322, 3300 AH Dordrecht, The Netherlands.

ISBN 0-7923-8942-5

Copyright

Published in the United Kingdom by Kluwer Academic Publishers, P.O. Box 55, Lancaster, U.K.

Kluwer Academic Publishers BV incorporates the publishing programmes of D. Reidel, Martinus Nijhoff, Dr W. Junk and MTP Press.

Origination by Roby Education Ltd, Liverpool.

Printed in Gt. Britain by Butler and Tanner Ltd., Frome and London.

Contents

Foreword

General Practice is undergoing the most major series of changes since the introduction of the National Health Service in 1948. They concern both concepts of care and practical details of the way care is delivered. In spite of the hostility generated by the changes most of the broad general concepts have been accepted. The principle of patients having more choice is widely supported, the inclusion of preventive medicine and anticipatory care in the responsibilities of practice has few opponents, the introduction of audit as a way of improving performance has been generally welcomed. Even the idea of putting GPs in better financial management of patients and drug budgets has had supporters in principle. The antipathy has generally related to the method of introduction of these changes. One important concern has been the time requirements of the New Contract and the feeling that these will erode the real nature of our work: the close personal relationship with patients.

If we improve the quality of our management this is less likely to happen. We shall be able to work within the New Contract and retain the quality of service we provide. If we improve the understanding of our staff of what we are trying to achieve we are more likely to reach the targets that we set whilst keeping people happy.

This book sets out to explain the New Contract. An understanding of this will be essential to those of us who have to work the system, and if we are better informed it will give us more chance of making the sensible amendments that will certainly be needed. I believe it will be a highly valuable source of information for Principals, Trainees and staff in practice and very strongly commend it.

Professor Sir Michael Drury
Head, Department of General Practice
University of Birmingham Medical School

Chapter 1

Organisation for What ?

To organise effectively and economically, it is necessary to understand what organisation is for and what aims, goals and targets are to be set.

WHAT IS PRIMARY HEALTH CARE (PHC) ?

"Primary Health Care" is the term adopted by the World Health Organisation to denote the first levels of care carried out in a health system. It includes community care, personal care, family care, together with curative, preventative and health promotional care.

It is necessary to be more precise. In any national health care system there are four levels of health care.

Fig 1.1
Levels of care

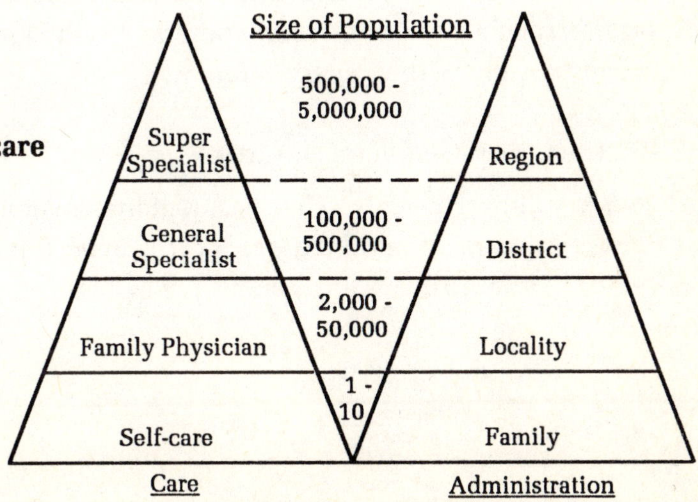

Self Care

Self Care is the largest first level of care in the context of a family. Three quarters of all symptoms and minor injuries are dealt with at this level without involving doctors or other health professionals.

It is important in any organisation delivering care that families and individuals should be encouraged and assisted to carry out suitable self care, promote their own good health and collaborate with professionals.

Primary Professional Care

Primary Professional Care is not only the level of general medical practice, but also of other general community care by trained nurses, midwives, health visitors, social workers and other trained persons.

Secondary General Specialist Care

Secondary General Specialist Care is that carried out at district general hospitals. It is the level of general physicians, general surgeons, general paediatricians, general OBG specialists, general psychiatrists, general orthopaedic and trauma specialists together with others. It is the level which relates closely with primary care.

Tertiary Super-specialist Care

Tertiary Super-specialist Care is at regional level with units providing care for populations of 1 - 5 million through referrals from primary and secondary levels.

PRIMARY PROFESSIONAL CARE

Primary Professional Care is an essential level of health care that carries out particular roles and functions that have to be recognised and supported. These are similar in any health system although the details of administrative arrangements may vary.

Thus, in Britain, it is the general practitioner who is the doctor in primary medical care. In the USA it may be one of a collection of "specialoids" of interests - a paediatrician, an OBG, a family physician, a psychiatrist or from some other group. In the USSR it is a generalist "uchastok" (neighbourhood) doctor to whom patients are allocated.

Where there is no sound recognisable and acceptable level of primary medical care then that level of care becomes the responsibility of the local hospital.

The roles of primary medical care must be to:

- provide direct available access to patients on a 24 hour basis
- provide first contact care, including diagnostic assessment and management
- provide long term continuous, personal and family care, if possible via the same doctor/patient relationship
- work in a relatively small and static community. In western-type developed societies there is now one primary care doctor to cater for the needs of 2000 people
- carry out comprehensive care for a special collection of morbidity work that inevitably has a predominance of minor ailments, a sizeable proportion of chronic disorders and only a small number of acute major life-threatening emergencies

The functions of such doctors must be to provide much more than available services for minor and chronic diseases; they must be to go out and promote better health and prevent disease in the small communities for which they are responsible.

These doctors have important functions as protectors of the local hospitals from inappropriate cases and protectors of patients from unnecessary hospital care through an effective gatekeeping referral system.

These doctors have to act as coordinators and manipulators of available local community and medical resources for the benefit of their patients. This is a special skill that has to be developed and acquired by a doctor over the years whilst becoming acquainted with the potentials and abilities of local specialties and facilities.

"I'm just off out to promote better health and prevent disease in our small community, Mrs Simpkins."

The care expected can be divided into:

- clinical care involving the traditional process of diagnostic assessment and applying "cure sometimes, relief often and comfort always"
- supportive social care through the practice team or by enlisting other agencies
- preventive care through the efforts of the practice
- health promotional care by educating and stimulating individuals and families and by improving the local environment

WHAT IS BRITISH GENERAL PRACTICE ?

General practice is the British form of primary medical care. It has evolved over the centuries (see Book 1) and has been subject to major changes over the past 25 years.

Under the National Health Service general practice is recognised as a special field of medical practice with its own administration, regulations and responsibilities.

General practitioner principals are required to undergo an approved period of vocational training and although, in theory, GPs work as independent contractors, by contracts with local NHS Family Practitioner Committees (FPC), they are, in reality, an integral part of the NHS with ever increasing directives and controls.

Through their contract with FPCs, general practitioners accept the responsibility of providing 24 hour services to all patients registered with them. These services have increased through the New Contract of 1990.

Nevertheless, British general practice is still able to organise its premises and its work as it thinks best in meeting these responsibilities, and through this is receiving remuneration from the NHS.

Changes 1965 - 1990

Over the past 25 years, British general practice has radically changed (see also Book 1). It has moved on from a disparate cottage industry of about 20,000 separate units to an organised collection of some 8,000 medium and larger businesses each requiring increasing degrees of management and organisational skills.

The major changes from the Charter of 1965 to the Contract of 1990 have been:

- increasing numbers of NHS GP - principals (Table 1.1)
- decreasing list sizes (average per GP) (Table 1.2)
- mandatory vocational training with 3250 GP trainers and 2279 trainees in 1989
- larger group practices. More than 1 in 3 practices now have more than 5 GPs and the average size of practice is some 4 GP principals providing care for about 8,000 patients
- the concept of the Practice Team has developed rapidly with almost 1.5 whole time equivalent reimbursed employed staff per GP. However, most of these are part timers. Therefore, in 1990, the average practice team will look like Table 1.4
- Health Centres are increasing in numbers. In Scotland and Northern Ireland about half of GPs work from Health Centres
- the work load has increased per GP based on estimates from increasing annual consultation rates per person from General Household Surveys

Table 1.1 Numbers of NHS GP - principals

1965	1975	1985	1990
24,650	25,406	28,580	33,100

(increasing by 1.75% per year)

Table 1.2 List sizes (average per GP)

1965	1975	1985	1990
2243	2291	2140	1900

Table 1.3 Practice Group of GPs (%)

	1965	1990
Solo	23.0	10.0
x2	25.0	14.8
x3	25.5	18.5
x4	14.8	18.0
x5	6.5	16.9
x6 & over	5.2	21.8
	100.0	100.0

Table 1.4 The Average Practice Team in 1990

GP Principals	4
Trainee	1
Practice Nurse	1
Practice Manager	1
Receptionists/Secretaries	10
Cleaners	4
Total	21

Table 1.5 Number of Health Centres

	1965	1990
No. of Health Centres (est)	910	1525
% GPs working in Health Centres	20%	30%
1990 figures for: Scotland 40%	N. Ireland 52%	

Table 1.6 Increase in Workload

	1965	1990
List Size	2243	1900
Annual Consultations per person	3	5
Annual Consultations per GP	6729	9500
Consultations per GP per week	135	190
Consultations per GP per day	27	38

WHAT IS "GOOD GENERAL PRACTICE" ?

What then is "good general practice" and how can it be organised? From the preceding data and comments, it is evident, with practice units caring for an average of 8,000 patients, by practice teams of 20, that organisation has to be a high priority.

Objectives must be to provide:

- available and accessible service
- personal family care
- high satisfaction for patients and practice team
- long term care in a stable practice team for a stable population so that each gets to know each other
- good communications and provision of information
- comprehensive care within the competence of the Practice
- high quality and standards based on agreed protocols which are monitored and checked by reliable, easily collected data which can be analysed and implemented to achieve changes for improvement
- good relations and contact with others in the local health service i.e. hospitals and community services

TARGETS AND GOALS

The Practice has to be well organised so as to achieve best use of available resources in most effective, efficient and economic ways, with regular evaluations.

In general terms, good organisation should be concerned with:

- **Structure** : A sound structure of the Practice including acceptable premises with good management and administration.

- **Processes** : Processes of care which should be agreed by the Practice Team and facilitated through acceptable protocols and guidelines.
- **Outcomes** : Outcomes of care should be under constant review to decide what is useful and beneficial against what is useless, unnecessary and with potential risks and dangers
- **Costs** : These should be monitored and controlled to achieve best value for money. This should include attention to more mundane home economics of the Practice, as well as to budgets related to prescribing, referrals and other matters.

In addition to these general organisational principles, under the New Contract, "targets" have to relate to measurable levels of achieving child immunisation and cervical cytology rates, also in carrying out other specified tasks (see Book 1).

The following chapters will detail the organisation in a practice which is necessary to carry out good general practice in the fields of clinical care, social care, prevention of disease, relations with others, communications, data recording and analysis, education and training.

Chapter 2

Clinical Care and Services

Services in general practice can be divided broadly into three main categories: clinical care, preventative health promotion and social support.

However, every patient contact may include all three in various degrees and the involvement may extend into family and community care, as well as that of the individual.

WHAT IS CLINICAL CARE ?

Patients see clinical care as the main priority. They interpret it as traditional care, relief and comfort for their symptoms, discomforts and disabilities.

The nature of clinical problems in general practice mirrors that of expected morbidity. Firstly there is a preponderance of minor, benign and self limiting conditions. Secondly there are a significant number of chronic persisting disorders for which there are no "cures" and which require long term and continuing care. Thirdly there is a small minority of major and life threatening situations to which the GP has to be ready to respond.The proportions are shown in Figure 2.1. Good organisation has to meet all various conditions.

Fig 2.1 Morbidity grades in general practice

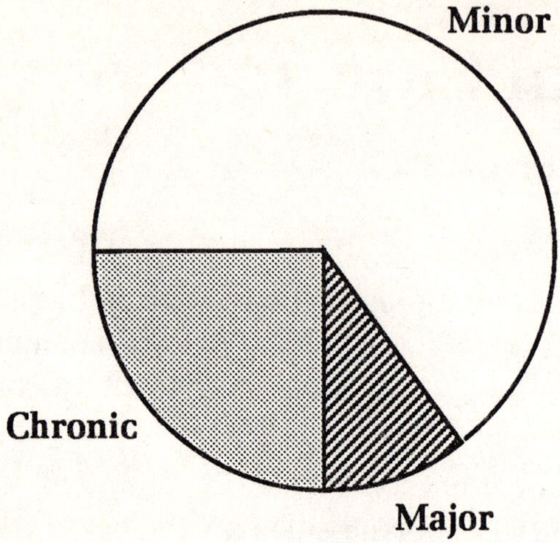

How to organise

The aims of practice organisation are to provide services that are:

- available
- accessible
- comprehensive
- personal (including concern, interest, understanding and explanation)
- continuing
- measurable
- changeable
- satisfactory and satisfying (for patient, doctor and NHS!)

All this with suitable premises, facilities, resources and staffing.

What to provide ?

GP services for patients can be divided into well defined sectors:

- surgery (office) consultations
- home visits
- special clinics and similar services
- out of hours cover
- other professional work (outside of the practice)

For these to be provided in comfort and without unnecessary stress, adequate premises have to be provided with appropriate space and facilities.

The proportionate amount of time a typical GP will spend each week on these various activities (Table 2.1) shows that consultations are the largest component.

Table 2.1 A GP's week in hours

Type of Work	Hours
Consultations	30
Home visits	10
Special clinics	3
Administration	5
Outside work	2
Total	50
plus on call	18
Total	68

Consultations

Consultations at the Practice premises are the largest part of the work. The patterns, methods and customs of provision are basically similar, with local variations in each practice.

Some truisms should be noted:

- general practice is essentially a long term clinic with continuity for a fairly static and stable population so that each consultation is a follow up of contact

- since this is so, the length of each consultation can be 5 - 10 minutes. There is nothing wrong in this because there is no need to start from scratch each time getting to know the patient and background

- access and availability are important and barriers should be avoided by having a pleasant reception service with minimal delays. It should be noted that receptionists are in the shop window of the Practice

- It is important that patients and practice staff know the system and how to operate it effectively. Clearly written information and instructions are necessary so the room for error is minimised.

Appointments or no appointments ?

Appointments for consultations have become a feature in general practice only since the early 1970s. Before it was open-sesame, with long queues and waiting periods. Now, even with appointment systems, patients may wait to see a doctor at time for as long as 30 minutes to 1 hour (N.B. appointments for hospitals OPDs were unknown before 1950).

The pros of appointments

- for patients are avoidance of uncertain long waits and opportunity to fix an appointment for a convenient time

- for GPs are planned control of consultations with known finishing times, fitting the length of consultation times to meet patient's requirements and the flexibility to make other future arrangements

The cons of appointments

- for patients are the inconvenience and costs of having to make an appointment, the wait for an appointment to see the doctor of choice, the occasional delays and excessive waiting time when the system gets behind. It is important to note that patients are less tolerant of "waits" within an appointment system than with a free-for-all system

- for GPs are the extra organisation required with extra cost of staffing, telephone and records, the problems of blocked telephone lines and patients unable to get a reply for some time, problems of fitting in "emergencies" on the same day or "non-emergencies" for doctors of choice with 24 - 48 hours and problems of unpredictability of how long a consultation will take

"That's a point! You *might* be dead in three week's time. In case this happens could you make prior arrangements for somebody to ring in and cancel the appointment!"

An effective appointment system requires data on the numbers of patients likely to be seen and for how long. Knowing this, some simple calculations can be made:

- the average number of consultations per person in a single year is 4 - 5. Therefore knowing the list size, the approximate number of weekly consultations can be calculated. With a patient list of 2,000 a doctor can expect to hold 8000 - 10000 consultations per year. Divided by 50 weeks yields an approximate 160 - 200 per week. It follows that for a five day week there will be 32 - 40 consultations each day

- alternatively, the number of consultations can be recorded over a 4 week period and then averaged

- next, the length of time of a consultation should be averaged since some are bound to be longer than others. Supposing that the average length of consultation is approximately 8 minutes, the doctor can expect to see 7 - 8 patients per hour

- therefore, the 32 daily consultations will take 4 hours, or 2 sessions of 2 hours. The 40 consultations will take 5 hours.

With this knowledge, arrangements can be made for a booking policy of, say, 3 patients every 20 minutes.

The same principle can be followed for the Practice Nurse appointments.

Attention should also be paid to:

- the telephone system - with appointments to be made the single line is likely to be blocked and a separate line for appointments may be necessary to be staffed by somebody specifically allocated to this role

- practice rules should be devised to cope with "emergencies" and demanding callers

- appointment books should be used and analysed periodically and other records kept of any problems which have obviously arisen

- preparation for each consulting session requires a system of having the medical record envelopes ready and stacked for each doctor, with a list of those booked in to the session

All these records may be given to the doctor at the start of the session or given to the patient who will, in turn, present them to the doctor.

Case Example

Appointment System - John Fry

- Introduced in 1964 after much uncertainty.
- A "complete" system was used from the start
- There was relative chaos for only a few weeks - patients appreciated the innovation
- Changes required
    - extra receptionists
    - extra telephone lines
    - appointment book (obtained from Lloyd Harnol & supplied free)
    - new attitudes to patients

- Principles evolved
    - find out average consulting time per GP
    - establish average number of consultations per GP
    - book at these rates and for appropriate time but leave gaps for "emergencies"

- doctors must always be prepared to "fit in" patients
- receptionists must be informed of any likely extra long consultations in advance
- appointment book must be marked off in advance for sessions to be crossed out when GP will be away
- appointment system should also be used for practice nurse and other clinics
- although, in theory, there should be a minimal waiting time for patients this still averages 10 - 15 minutes.
- we would never go back to a no-appointment system

Case Example

Appointment / Non-Appointment System - Kenneth Scott

- The Practice introduced an Appointment/Non-appointment system in 1972
- Consultations each morning Monday - Saturday, patients seen without an appointment
- Consultations afternoon and evening by appointment
- A new appointment telephone line installed and the introduction of an appointment book
- The philosophy behind the introduction of this scheme is to give patients the opportunity to consult within 24 hours of complaint.
- Patient have the choice of waiting their turn in an open surgery or attending by appointment.
- Open morning surgeries offer flexibility to children being seen before school and adults on their way to work.

Advantages to the Practice

- Most consultations for acute conditions are seen in an open surgery.
- A reduction in the number of patients requesting urgent appointments or home visits.

- More time available in appointment sessions for longer consultations.

Disadvantages

- Records have to be pulled at the time of attendance, so requiring an extra member of staff.

Comment

Experience shows that attendances at open surgeries are remarkably constant which does not interfere with the doctor planning his/her day. Open surgeries are for general medical conditions only. Appointment clinics in operation for all specialist services e.g. Maternity, Family Planning, Well Person etc.

At the conclusion of a consultation, arrangements should be made for a follow up appointment should one be necessary. It is estimated that between one half to two thirds of initial appointments will require a follow up appointment to be made.

Should this follow up appointment be made to be in a few days, 2, 3 or 4 weeks, or in 2 or 3 months? Naturally it will depend on clinical circumstances, but attention should be given as to whether a re-appointment is too soon or too late. The timing depends on how far the appointment book is made up!

Another matter to contend with is that of the non attenders. In many practices this is not a big problem, there being an incidence of approximately 1 in 10 or less. However, some practices do experience it as a particular problem with the incidence being as high as 1 in 4. Such a situation may be welcome if one is running late, but not if it leads to empty gaps. Apart from noting the non attendance (DNA = did not attend) in the notes, and taking up the matter subsequently, there are no penalties that can be levied under the NHS.

REPEAT PRESCRIPTIONS

This has become an integral part of NHS practice organisation. Each year there are 7 - 8 prescriptions for each person. With an annual face to face consultation rate of 4 - 5, this means an annual rate of 3 - 4 repeat prescriptions per person. It may be more because a prescription is issued in only 60% - 70% of consultations.

Therefore, if there are 32 - 40 daily consultations there may be as many as 20 - 30 repeat prescriptions to be issued daily.

The methods used by practices vary. Most repeat prescriptions are prepared by the receptionists and signed by the GP (NB issue of pre-signed blank prescriptions is professionally illegal) but they can also be computerised.

Case Example

Repeat Prescriptions - John Fry

- If all patients had to be seen for a prescription, this would add 3 - 4 hours consulting time per day.
- A manual system is used.
- Patients 'phone (after 11 a.m.) or send a note for script to be picked up, or a stamped addressed envelope to be posted.
- No special request cards are used.
- Receptionists get out patient's NHS medical records, prepare prescription form with name, address and drug entered.

- GP must see records, enter the repeats in notes, check and sign each script (write out script completely for listed drugs).
- "Repeats" take up at least an hour daily.

Case Example - Kenneth Scott

The development of the use of computers in general practice has revolutionised the process of issuing repeat prescriptions.

Once the information is recorded on the computer it needs to be regularly updated according to change of medication, which will then serve as a reliable source of generating accurate prescriptions.

Advantages

- Accurate legible prescriptions
- Generic prescribing
- Ease with which patients can request their next prescription by using the tear off slip attached to the prescription
- Computer printed prescriptions eliminate the risk of alterations
- Practice audit on prescribing can be undertaken
- Check on the number of prescriptions issued
- Drug interactions can be identified

Essentially, a "repeat prescription" or, more accurately, one for an "unseen patient", should be recorded in the patient's notes. Some guidelines should exist for regular reviews of such patient's requests.

HOME VISITS

In the NHS, home visiting is part of the GP's terms of service. It has always been an integral part of general practice although now there is much less home visiting than there was before the 1930s. Then it was accepted that a GP with 2000 patients would carry out 20 - 30 home visits a day, but see only 20 - 30 patients in the consulting room, which was usually situated in the doctor's home. Now a GP with similar numbers of patients will make visits to only 2 - 5 patients each day in their homes.

Nevertheless, home visiting still accounts for about 20% of the GP's work time. The patient expects the doctor to visit and "failure or refusal to visit" is the most frequent complaint made against GPs and the most likely reason for Medical Service Committee hearings. Such complaints may be passed on to the General Medical Council if found proved and serious.

Why and what for ?

There are three reasons for home visits:

1. A new request - to visit a sick person who is unable, or not prepared, to come to the Practice premises. These patients have illnesses ranging from minor upper respiratory infections or gastrointestinal upsets to life threatening emergencies such as myocardial infarctions, surgical abdominal emergencies and strokes.

It is in the latter situations that the dangers in non response by a GP can occur. It is dangerous to diagnose "acute indigestion" in a middle aged man with chest pain. If it turns out to be be a myocardial infarction then the GP might be in serious trouble. Likewise, refusal to visit a feverish child who may, against the odds, have a meningitis or one with a croupy cough who turns out to have epiglottitis, and so on.

The basic rule must be for the GP to "visit first and moan later". It often happens that requests which one is reluctant to respond to turn out to be the most necessary.

2. A follow up of a new request - this used to be a frequent reason for visiting before the availability of oral antibiotics and other effective specific drugs. Patients with infections had to be visited almost daily to assess progress.

Now follow up visits are indicated when initial diagnosis and assessment are uncertain as in possible "acute abdomens", "pneumonias", "TIAs" and feverish children.

3. Regular visits to patients with chronic conditions, such as severe arthritis, neurological disorders, COAD, or more general disabilities of old age are reasons for a social medical visit from the GP. The social benefits for the patients are greater than their medical needs. The frequency of such visits may be weekly, monthly or quarterly. These visits may be shared with nurses but not handed over completely.

Who to do home visits ?

Home visiting is now shared with district nurses, practice nurses and midwives. Each patient should have guidelines as to who will be doing the visiting and how frequently the visiting will take place.

Although it is possible for a nurse to make a first visit in response to a new request, it is fraught with medico-legal problems. The GP should respond personally to all new requests.

It is acceptable practice for a nurse to carry out follow up and chronic visiting but there should always be close liaison and consultation between doctor and nurse.

How to allocate

Arrangements for allocation vary with practices:

- In some, the GP with whom the patient is registered, or who is asked for, will be expected to visit.

- In others, allocation is determined geographically and certain areas of the Practice may be visited by particular GPs on certain days and new visits will be passed on to them.

- In larger practices GPs may have a daily rota - one may do all the home visits on that day.

Response to requests

Clear guidelines should be set in each practice on how the doctor or receptionist respond:

- The receptionist must not be expected to refuse a request. It is acceptable to "encourage" patients to come to the surgery, but no more.

- Either the request is accepted at once or the call should be passed on to the doctor to deal with the matter on the telephone.

- Requests should be recorded in a book noting accurately the patient's name, address, telephone number and reason for the request. The timing of the request should also be noted.

- The patient's clinical records should be presented to the GP who should take these on the visit and enter notes at the time of the visit.

OUT-OF-HOURS SERVICES

The NHS GP is contractually obliged to provide 24 hour care and cover for registered patients. Historically this has always been the custom.

Before the NHS (pre 1948) most GPs were in solo practice and most of their patients were "private" or fee paying. (Some were "panel patients" i.e. manual low paid workers covered under National Health Insurance). There was active and fierce competition for patients and GPs tended to be on call 24 hours a day, 7 days a week.

"Let's just say it's Dr. Hayes' Christmas present!"

Over the years there has been a growth of group practice and now only 1 in 10 of GPs is single handed, and over half work in groups of 4 or more. This has led to a sharing of work, including out-of-hours services.

What is it and why ?

Organisation of GP work now is through a busy daytime routine of consultations, home visits, other tasks and sharing of out-of-hours work.

"Out-of -hours" implies evening and night time work, usually from 6 pm to 8 am and weekends over Friday, Saturday, Sunday and public holidays. In addition, there may be in-practice arrangements to cover for outside work and holidays etc.

Who does it ?

Various arrangements exist:

- Self cover is a solo practice with the GP on call all the time. This is most unusual but does occur in small isolated units.

- In-practice cover where the partners make mutual arrangements between themselves.

- Local rotas between a number of practices.

- Commercial deputising services - in heavily populated areas these exist and many GPs, including those in the above systems, arrange for their out-of-hours work to be covered by these organisations (under the New Contract FPCs have to approve these arrangements and there are variable payments for night visits - 10 pm - 8 am for those done by commercial deputising services and GPs themselves).

How to organise

Whatever system is used, an efficient organisation is most important.

Careful attention is necessary for:

- ensuring that the patients know what to do to obtain services - notices at practice premises, practice leaflets, answerphone
- ensuring the doctor on call is fully aware that he/she is on call
- ensuring that the communication system works! It should be as simple and as clear as possible
- ensuring that a telephone system gives an adequate response. Ideally this should not involve too much re-routing with the patient having to make many 'phone calls

The possibilities are:

- member of staff personally answering and routing all calls
- commercial answer call service
- direct transfer to doctor on call
- answerphone message (always make a test call)

It is important to log and record all messages and calls received as these may be necessary in answering complaints.

Have a standard form of response to requests including:

- name, age, address, 'phone number
- patient's GP
- reason for call and service requested
- response - visit to be done - arrange to see at practice - premises or hospital, advice given

ROTA LISTS

Any rota of GPs requires an agreed table setting out date on which individuals are on call.

Case Example - Kenneth Scott

- Rotas may involve the doctors of more than one practice as the current GP contract allows up to 10 doctors to cover for each other.
- The rota should be planned a year ahead and should be the responsibility of one member of the rota team.
- A rota will be efficient and reliable once an agreed protocol has been established and agreed by all doctors taking part in the rota. Changes to the protocol can only be made by agreement with all concerned.

Doctors need to agree:

- the times the rota will cover
- to see and treat all patients on the lists of doctors within the rota
- to personally inform the patient's doctor of any patient either admitted to hospital or who might need follow up consulatations either at home or at the surgery
- that any changes in duties in the established rota must be notified to all doctors taking part in the rota

Local Rota

- five doctors working in two practices. Each doctor has a set "on call" night per week, Monday - Friday.

- one doctor is "on call" one weekend in five from Saturday midday to 7 a.m. Monday morning

- Christmas and Bank Holidays are excluded from the routine rota

- a separate rota operates for Christmas and Bank Holidays when each practice alternates the "on call" cover

- regular fixed nights for week day "on call" may be inconvenient, but changes in the rota can be arranged at the time the rota is drawn up

- weekend and Bank Holiday rotas can be extended to other practices which can be operated independently from the weekend rota, so long as agreed protocol is adhered to and does not include more than 10 doctors

OUTSIDE WORK

It is likely that GPs involved in regular outside (out of practice) activities are happier and better GPs.

Therefore, some outside work should be encouraged, provided that GPs still meet their requirements of work hours stated. (See Book 1).

The scope is extensive:

- National professional organisations

  GMC
  BMA
  RCGP

- Local professional organisations
  - Health Authority
  - FPC
  - LMC
  - College faculty
  - BMA division
- Professional work
  - Hospital appointments
  - Insurance work
  - Occupational medicine
  - Sports medicine
- Education and training
  - Trainer-trainee medical students,
  - Postgraduate medical education
- Research
  - In-practice,
  - Collaborative
- Personal hobbies and interests

Case Example - John Fry

- Some "outside work" is good for GPs and their patients.
- Each GP develops a particular interest and schedule.
- My own personal schedule is one that interferes minimally with practice work.
- Reading (papers), writing (papers, books etc), research recording and analysis is carried out in my "own time" - early morning (I get up at 5 a.m.) or evenings (I go to bed at 11 p.m.) and at weekends.

- I arrive at the practice premises before 7 a.m. and leave at 6 p.m.
- Thursday is my regular "meeting day" when I see people in London and elsewhere (after morning practice work).
- GMC work is mostly by post - there are two Council meetings a year (over 2 days). Committee meetings I try to arrange on a Thursday!
- Editorial meetings are also fitted in on a Thursday.
- LMC & BMA (local) meetings are in the evenings.
- RCGP Council meetings now are every 2 months on alternate Friday/Saturday.
- Dates of formal meetings are usually known many months in advance and arrangements can be made with partners and for non-booking of appointments.
- In the past (many years ago) when I was single handed I served as a surgical clinical assistant for two sessions a week.

Case Example - Kenneth Scott

It is possible for a general practitioner to undertake commitments outside the Practice and still provide a maximum commitment to patients and colleagues.

The amount of time committed will depend upon the individual practitioners interests and the time they are prepared to allow to other commitments and how much of their leisure time they are prepared to sacrifice.

Example of outside commitment: Part Time Manager of Community Health Service

- Five sessions are required to undertake this commitment.
- Sessions can be arranged to start after morning surgeries or continue into the afternoons with me sacrificing practice half days.
- To compensate for afternoon sessions I undertake longer evening surgeries.

"*Of course* we like to encourage hobbies in this Practice, but one or two patients have complained..."

Also

- I represent my GP colleagues on the Legal Medical Committee of FPC and BMA Council meetings which are all held in the evenings.

- I attend District Health Authority Meetings, also in the evenings.

Obviously for GPs to be able to be involved in such activities, there have to be compromises and agreements with partners on working duties and availability to patients.

Chapter 3

Personal - Family - Social Care

Good general practice is much more than good clinical care. The individual patient, the family and the local community must be considered and served.

AIMS

In this wider context come:

- promotion of personal and family care involving mutual respect and understanding
- encouragement of continuity of care over many years by the same practice
- provision of support for social problems and appropriate use of available facilities and resources
- the Practice involved as part of the local community

How to organise ?

There are no "best buys" and no single overall ways of providing optimal personal and family social care.

Each practice has to evolve its own philosophies and policies but with attention to defined objectives.

This chapter looks at some issues that should be considered.

Personal or Practice Doctor?

It has to be fundamentally decided whether there should be a policy that each GP should have a "personal list" of patients who should be encouraged, whenever possible, to consult and to visit personal patients, the idea being that of reinforcing the one-to-one relationship.

Alternatively, it may be that the Practice decides to adopt the "Practice Doctor" policy where patients are encouraged to regard the Practice as a whole and the patients should be prepared to see whichever doctor or nurse is available.

Both methods can probably provide equally good standards of care.

In the first case the impact on practice organisation is considerable, requiring attention to appointments and visits being directed to particular doctors for particular patients.

Some very large practices split into smaller in-practice teams of GP - nurse - receptionist to provide more personal care.

Case Example - John Fry

- Practice policy (now 3 partners) has always been to provide "personal doctoring" for "own patients".

- I was single handed 1947-62 which allowed total personal doctoring - patients had no choice.

- One essence of good general practice is long term continuing same doctor-patient care over many years.

- Patients seeking appointments or home visits are always asked "Who is your doctor?" and efforts are made to ensure care by their doctor.

- We do not insist on this and allow patients to change around between partners and they are always free to chose.

Continuity of care

A special feature, and opportunity, of general practice is continuity of care. This should also lead to better understanding and offers the chance to observe and study the outcome of disease in man and of man coping with disease.

For this to be possible clinical records need to be arranged, organised, presented and legibly summarised so that they are easy to follow.

Case Example - John Fry

- Continuity of care offers great opportunities to GP.

- To study the natural history of common diseases in my practice I devised, in 1950, a very simple system of disease recording or indexing.

- An indexed notebook edged "A-Z" is in my desk drawer - each (or 2) letter can be used for a specific disease- such as high blood pressure, "I.H.D.", "cancers", "peptic ulcers", asthma, "anaemias" etc.

- As each new case is diagnosed the patient's name is entered into the book and then names and clinical details are regularly entered into card index boxes, one for each disease.

- Of course, it should be much easier now to use computerisation to achieve what I have been doing for 40 years!

Social Support

Although part of any consultation should consider the patient's social problems, if present, and they should be noted with sympathy, concern and understanding - there are limits to significant and realistic assistance.

The most prevalent social problems involve housing, shortage of money, interpersonal difficulties, personality weakness and coping with the problems of the elderly and the handicapped.

To be of assistance the Practice must create a core of knowledge and experience of available local facilities and resources that are available and establish links with useful organisations and people.

A member of the Practice Team, usually the Practice Nurse or Health Visitor, should be deputed to create a register and act as link person to whom other members of the Practice can turn.

Community Involvement

In smaller, well defined localities general practice plays important roles as a health promoter and disease preventer, as well as a clinical carer. Members of the Practice should be prepared to become involved in, and help organise, such activities.

Chapter 4

Disease Prevention and Health Promotion ?

The Contract seeks to encourage and reward disease prevention and health promotion. Organisation for these activities requires thoughtful planning. In this chapter the various sectors are dealt with in respect of:

- why undertake - aims and objectives
- what and how should it be done?
- who should do it?
- evaluation

ANTENATAL CARE

Although not specifically included in the Contract it is an important activity that sets the scene for the others.

Why?

- care for expectant mothers in the Practice - usually shared with local obstetric unit

- content traditionally seeks to pick up early any abnormalities that will need attention

- to involve the Practice attached midwife and health visitor

- to prepare the mother for pregnancy and use the contacts for more general health promotion, with the health visitor preparing her for health care generally and for arrangements in the practice

- to build up good patient-practice team relationships

What and how ?

The antenatal visit should include the normal consultation, examination, weight and blood pressure checks, urinalysis by the doctor and midwife and also a separate consultation with the health visitor.

With the annual birth rate of 13 per 1000, each GP can expect to deal with 26 births in any given year and organisation has to relate to these numbers.

All or one GP ?

It may be that antenatal care is carried out by each GP partner or delegated to one or more GPs in larger practices. If the latter system is used, then the GP-mother relationship is not developed.

Separate sessions ?

If the stated aims are to be achieved then antenatal care sessions should be held separately from the rest of the practice health promotional clinics.

Timing will depend on how many expectant mothers are expected to attend and indeed how often they will attend. Generally a monthly appointment is appropriate, bearing in mind that she will be seen a couple of times at the hospital obstetric unit whilst early in the pregnancy and more frequently as the time for confinement approaches.

If possible 1 or 2 hours should be allocated to the clinic, its frequency depending on the numbers to be seen. Naturally the time and date must be suitable for patient, doctor, midwife and health visitor.

Records

A co-operation card with entries by GPs and hospitals and held by the patient is now customary, but these vary between units. In addition, it is recommended that the GP also retains a personal copy of the obstetric card.

"Yes, we *did* send a letter to encourage good record keeping, but...."

Evaluation

It is useful periodically for the team to meet and discuss:

- whether arrangements are satisfactory - taking note of patient's views
- co-operation with hospital
- any recent clinical problems
- results of pregnancies

Case Example - John Fry

- Diagnosis of pregnancy is made at regular practice consultation
- Pregnancy tests are rarely necessary if the patient can give the necessary explanation
- Appointment is made to attend antenatal clinic
- At the first ANC attendance necessary records are completed and a referral letter written to obstetrician
- ANC is held every 2 weeks on a Monday 12.30 pm - 2.30 pm.
- 10 - 15 patients are seen at each clinic
- Monthly appointment for patient unless greater frequency felt to be necessary
- GP and midwife to see patient jointly
- Health visitor consultation follows
- Co-op card used and completed together with RCGP green obstetric card
- Following delivery, mother and baby seen at home by midwife and GP, if necessary (some GPs visit routinely)
- Mother is expected to attend Children Clinic at the Practice when the baby is 2 - 3 weeks old
- Mother attends for postnatal examination at 8 weeks.

NEW REGISTRATIONS TO THE PRACTICE

GPs are expected to carry out health checks on all patients joining their lists who are over the age of 5 years provided the patient did not have a similar consultation from an existing partner in the previous 12 months.

Invitations to attend the practice for screening can be made verbally but should be confirmed in writing and have to be made within 28 days of the patient being accepted onto the list.

Details of consultation must include:

- Medical history
- Social history
- Life-style
- Current state of health
- Physical examination - height, weight, blood pressure, urinalysis

Examination is expected to be carried out within three months of the patient joining the list although provision allows this to be extended to 12 months if the practitioners can demonstrate that the examination took place at the first opportunity.

Patients usually consult their medical practitioner when seeking general medical advice for a specific condition and some patients may be reluctant to attend for a specific screening check although these appointments should be offered at times convenient to the patient.

It is appropriate to undertake screening opportunistically at the time of the first consultation and this can be completed by the GP at the end of the consultation or by the Practice

Nurse. The proposed standard form for this examination should be included in the patient's medical record.

Some practices may find it more appropriate to allocate specific clinic times for all new entrants and attend for consultation as a family unit.

Practices should establish a protocol for the screening programme which should be adhered to by all members of the primary care team.

CHILD SURVEILLANCE

Child surveillance can be undertaken in general practice by the GP suitably qualified and recognised by the FPC.

- The initial appointment for the first screening check at six weeks should be arranged through the health visitor when visiting the mother at the postnatal visit.

- On attendance at the 6 week check the appropriate form, Number FP/CHS, should be completed and signed by the parent confirming the wish for the practice to undertake the child surveillance programme.

- The completion of the 6 week check should be entered into the medical record and that information transferred to the computer.

- The details of the medical examination should be completed by the doctor on form ——— which is sent to the Child Health Department of the District Health Authority.

- Also recorded on the child's record will be the entry that the parent has signed, the FP/CHS form and this detail is also entered on the Practice computer.

Children joining the practice between the ages of six weeks and five years

The parents of these children who join the list in these age bands should be asked to undertake their child's surveillance programme and if so Form FP/CHS can be completed when registering.

Confirmation of the signed form should be entered into the patients records and the practice computer.

ELDERLY

It is a requirement of the GP contract to screen patients over the age of 75 years on an annual basis. Such patients should be offered, if necessary, a home visit for this assessment.

Most patients over the age of 75 years are independent, active and responsible people who are proud of their independence. This independence should be encouraged. A high percentage of patients in this catagory, however, do have health care needs and as long as they are able they should be encouraged to visit the surgery. Health screening should be undertaken opportunistically as and when they visit the surgery.

Patients who are immobile or confined to their homes should be assessed by the professional member of the primary care team who holds the appropriate qualification. The assessment should be carried out in the patient's home using the nursing process agreed format. Included in the screening process, patients' needs should be identified and classified as either Medical or Social, so that they can be referred to the appropriate agency. Completion of opportunistic screening should be entered on the practice computer so that, at any given point, the Practice can identify those patients who have attended and completed their surveillance, as opposed to those who have not been seen. Contact needs to be made with these patients by either:

- A letter from the Practice inviting them to attend for screening.
- A letter offering a home visit with the appropriate member of the Primary Care Team being asked to visit the patient at home. This team member must wear an official identity badge with photograph.

Recent study, undertaken in general practice of 12,000 patients, showed that 10% of patients over the age of 75 years had not attended their doctor in the previous 12 months. Each of these patients was followed up either by a visit or a request asking them to attend the surgery. 5% of these were found to have social needs only.

THREE YEAR CHECKS

General practitioners are expected to offer consultation to every patient between the ages of 16 and 74 years, who have not attended the Practice during the preceding three years.

The establishment of a system whereby this can be determined is a formidable undertaking and can be achieved only by either keeping manual or computerised records.

Only by cross indexing those patients on the Practice List with those on the previously mentioned manual or computerised records will practices be able to identify those patients to whom letters should be written offering a consultation.

Practices which have not been keeping computerised records during the last three years will need to undertake manual inspection of all records in order to isolate patients who have not visited during the last three years. The information gleaned from the manual inspection can, in turn, be transferred to a computerised record. Those practices which are not computerised will need to keep careful manual records to readily identify relevant patients.

"Here's another old one, doctor.
'Mr. R. Biggs - last check-up 1963'.
I wonder what happened to him?"

The Practice needs to survey all records and place an appropriate marker, which can be easily identified (e.g. white card), into the patients record. This card should be marked with an appropriate colour for each year which will indicate the year of the last consultation - e.g. black 1987, blue 1988, red 1989 and yellow 1990.

This coding system will readily identify those patients who have not been seen during the required time scale. It is expected that by 1st April 1991 all patients not seen in the previous three years will have been identified.

The Practice will send an invitation to the patient to attend for screening which could be effected in a well man / well-woman session.

RECORDS

Patients' general practice medical records contain a wealth of data which has not been harnessed to give useful information. The new GP contract has highlighted the deficiency of not having available information about the status of patients' health.

There is no recommended format as to which data should be collected nor has there been a standard system of collection recommended by the Department of Health. Furthermore, there has not been any financial incentive offered to support the enormous administrative costs which will be incurred to meet the terms of the new Contract.

GPs and nurses have traditionally entered details of consultations and clinical data on the standard FP7,8. These details are filed in the record envelope and referred to as and when appropriate. Few practices have, to date, attempted to compile a disease summary for individual patients together with a medication chart, including all medication which is used exclusively for repeat prescriptions.

Computerisation in general practice has revolutionised data collection but the data recorded is not standardised and depends on individual practice requirements.

A disease index for each patient will need to be collected manually and recorded on the standard card. This standard card can also be used as a long term medication card which forms the basis from which a computerised record can be obtained and repeat prescriptions produced. Protocols need to be established in each practice to determine which data is included on the computer so that accuracy is ensured.

Manual inspection of records, no matter how well these records are organised, is a formidable and unreliable method of analysing data. Computerisation is essential for the future.

Data can be recorded at the time of consultation but this is time consuming and the operator needs to have the necessary keyboard skills.

Practical Point

It is imperative to mark the manual record with an appropriate sign against information which has been entered on the computer for further reference. Accuracy of data is paramount for providing reliable information essential for medical audit and the completion of administrative tasks required for the New Contract.

All specific information recorded on the computer can have an appropriate marker such as:

- new registrant
- dates of Child Surveillance examinations
- dates of last consultation
- cervical cytology
- elderly screening date
- clinical conditions.

The marker can then be called up at any time to give the information required to complete records.

Protocol on Recording Information

This will depend on the methods agreed by individual practices.

- Direct recording at the time of consultation by the doctor or the nurse. This will, of course, require there to be a VDU and a keyboard in the consulting room.
- Consultations recorded in the patient's record. This data is transferred into the computerised record by an input clerk.

COMMUNICATION

The future developments in primary care will necessitate improved communication between all agencies that are responsible for providing medical or social care in the district.

GPs no longer work in isolation in so much as they all employ ancilliary staff. Working relationships, within the practice setting, and between all disciplines are enhanced by:

- regular meeting with each professional group
- inter group meetings conducted in a somewhat social format such as a working lunch

Communication beyond the Practice is fundamental for future development of patient care, both in quality and quantity, and practices should maintain contact with Health Authorities, Local Authorities and Voluntary Organisations.

Beyond the Contract, the changes in the method of providing health care from April 1991, by the establishment of a commissioning health purchasing service from appropriate providers such as Health Authorities, Self Governing Trusts and the Private Sector, will necessitate a visibly improved communication system between general practice and the provider of services. This will ensure that patients are receiving the most appropriate medical care.

"Contract...contract...ah! Here it is.
It says 'An agreement only binding on the weaker party' "

Chapter 5

A Practice Directory-Relations With Others

General Practice cannot work in professional isolation. As the role of a GP is also that of a user of services he/she also has to function as a:

- co-ordinator
- manipulator
- facilitator
- protector (of hospital and other services from inappropriate patients and vice versa, of patients from inappropriate services)

One of the features of good care and one of the special skills in general practice is to know and relate to local situations and resources and how best to use them for the sake of patients.

The Practice Team should know:

- what services are available
- what these services have to offer
- how to contact them
- who can do what best
- how to communicate with individuals
- how best to react to past experiences

How to Organise and Record the Data and Information

Each practice should prepare its own fact-file directory of these services. Although the preparation, contents and composition of such a directory must be done by each practice individually, because experiences and relationships will vary, there are certain principles to be followed:

- the directory must be planned by all members of the Practice Team with each member making contributions. However, it should be prepared by one person such as the Practice Manager or one of the GPs
- the aims should be agreed
- the contents list with main sub divisions should be prepared and given to each member of the team to add items of detail
- the directory must be highly confidential to encourage incorporation of comments that may be entered on the various services and individuals
- the directory should be available to any member of the team who needs to refer to it (copies should be kept in the individual care of each GP)
- although a manual directory may be more feasible at present, it can be computerised and so give even greater attention to confidentiality

How to make it up

Having agreed on the need for a practice directory and on its general aims, the person delegated to compile the work should start work:

- to produce a classification of main subjects and sub-divisions

- to present suggestions on the lay out

- to propose whether it should be contained in a loose leaf binder or in a bound book with alphabetical edging such as an address book

- to produce drafts of possible entries

- to include in each entry information on: name of organisation or person, addresses and telephone numbers, the services provided, the name of the contact person and relevant comments as to the usefulness of what is on offer

Possible Contents

It is important to recognise that this exercise should be based on individual needs of practices but the check lists on pages 145 - 148 can be considered and, of course, added to or subtracted from.

"I know we're compiling a Practice Directory, but is there any need for you to refer to the section on jaundice as *The Yellow Pages*?"

HOSPITALS

Decisions have to be made on how much to include under each hospital. Local Hospital Authorities provide information on out-patient departments, consultant sessions and on various other services. These differ from area to area and it is helpful for practices to readjust some to make them more useful. Decisions have to be made as to whether the hospital leaflets should be included as they are, photocopied or amended. Decisions also have to be made on what and how many "comments" should be included.

Consultant

Because each practice generally relates to a relatively small number of consultants, good relations can readily be established. Therefore, it is no great task to list each consultant with personal details.

RELATIONS WITH OTHERS : General Practitioner/Hospital - The Future of Patient Care

The Government White Paper "Working for Patients" published in January 1989 identifies the future provision of patient care in that district services will be provided by a commissioning authority, and to achieve this a very close working relationship between general practitioner and hospital care must be developed.

It is paramount that GPs retain the right to refer their patients to the centre and to the consultant who they think can provide the best services for their patients' needs.

PERSONNEL

names, addresses and telephone numbers

Staff :
- doctors
- practice manager
- practice nurse
- secretary-receptionist
- others

Attached :
- district nurse
- health visitor
- midwife,
- social workers
- community psychiatric worker
- others

General :
- cleaners
- gardener
- odd job man
- others

Rota :
- details

Professional :
- bank
- accountant
- solicitor
- others

Map(s) :
- special notes
- new roads etc

PRACTICE & LOCAL SERVICES

Domestic Services	• telephone • heating • builder • plumber • electric • gas • water
Cars:	• garage • servicing • body repairs • others
Equipment Suppliers:	
(non-medical)	• typewriters etc. • computers • others
(office)	• printers • photocopying • stationery suppliers
(medical)	• drugs • surgical • medical • pharmaceutical companies notes on what is on offer
Voluntary :	• local organisations including national bodies and self help groups
Transport :	• trains • buses • taxis

PROFESSIONAL SERVICES

Local Practices :	• names of partners • others
Paramedical :	• pharmacies • physiotherapists • chiropodists • osteopaths • sports clinics • others
Local Authority :	• social workers • Social Services Dept. • Home Helps • Housing Dept. • Meals on Wheels • others
Social Security :	• local office • special services
Public Services :	• ambulance emergency • ambulance "cold cases" • private ambulance • police • coroner • district registrar
Representatives :	• Family Practitioner Committee • Medical Committee Post Graduate Medical Centre • Members of Parliament • Local Councillors

HOSPITALS / CLINICS / CONSULTANTS

NHS Hospital :

- Out-Patient departments (clinics, who, when, waiting times).
- admissions (arrangements, emergencies,cold admissions)
- Accident-Emergency,
- special services/ clinics.

Private Hospitals

Clinics for the termination of pregnancy

Nursing Homes

Homes for the elderly

Consultants

- speciality
- address
- telephone numbers (home & hospital)
- when and where available
- domicilliary availability
- special skills, comments

NATIONAL PROFESSIONAL ORGANISATIONS

General Medical Council
British Medical Association
Royal College of General Practitioners
Medical Defence Organisations
Royal Society of Medicine
others

However, the future of district hospitals depends on the maximum use that GPs are prepared to make of them in referring their patients for local services and reserving out-of-district referrals to those centres of excellence that provide specialist services.

To achieve the best services for our patients and ensure improved quality of care we need to be fully informed of the consultant staff working in the district. It is necessary to have knowledge of their:

- special interests within their consultancies
- out patient consulting details
- availability
- accessibility

Referral systems to hospital consultants vary in different districts and between different specialists and we should be acquainted with each system to minimise delay in patients being seen. Most specialists are prepared to see urgent cases in their clinics by direct contact. There is, however, a domicilliary visiting system available from consultants when appropriate.

Patients are referred to consultants for:

- an opinion about the presenting clinical condition and advice on further management
- investigations and continuing care
- possible hospital admission
- patient request for a second opinion

The type of referral that GPs will make in the future will, to some extent, be governed by the budget holding concept which is being introduced into general practice at the present time.

"You want a second opinion?
All right. You're ugly as well!"

Out-Patient Waiting Times

These are, nationally, unacceptably long. Mechanisms need to be developed by consultation with general practitioners and consultants as to how these waiting times can be dramatically reduced.

Incentives in the current GP Contract to make early diagnoses, promote disease prevention and develop surgical procedures are a step forward. However, local arrangements need to be made between general practice and those responsible for providing all hospital services to improve out-patient services.

Examples of How to Reduce Out-Patient Waiting Times

- Extend district investigating facilities which should include not only pathology and X-ray but also ultrasound investigation and mammography.
- Direct referral for remedial services e.g. physiotherapy and occupational therapy.

- Encourage earlier discharge so that GPs can undertake their own follow up care.
- Develop procedures within the primary care setting, e.g. minor surgery.
- Develop general practice follow up clinics, e.g. diabetes.

Admissions

The systems for emergency admissions to hospitals vary in different districts. The system could either be by :

- Direct consultation with the admitting medical officer.
- Through the district Admission Office or EBS.

Some districts have age-related admission policies for geriatric and psycho-geriatric patients. The age bands can vary in different districts and between each group.

The developing services in primary care are geared to complement those services provided in the community by the DHAs and Social Services. A closer working relationship should be established between all practitioners and their attached staffs.

The role of the health visitor is:

- health advice to expectant mothers
- advice and monitoring children 0 - 5 years
- child surveillance procedures
- assessment, monitoring and advice to the elderly
- advice on health to all age groups where appropriate

The health visitor undertakes work either in the Practice setting, community clinic or the patient's home.

The provision of assessment and surveillance of 75 year olds and others will require GPs to have a closer working relationship with members of the Primary Care Team which provides services for this age group.

Other services provided by the Community include :

- community psychiatric nurses who are either attached to general practice or consultant psychiatrists
- domicilliary physiotherapy
- domicilliary occupational therapy
- chiropody
- speech therapy
- dentistry

The future integration of primary care and community care is essential to support the Care in the Community concept that is proposed in the current Griffiths' document.

General Practitioner / Social Services

The Griffiths' White Paper "Care in the Community" strengthens the role of Local Authorities in the provision of social care.

The concept of the White Paper is to respect the wishes of individual clients and to ensure, where possible, and for however long it remains possible, for people to be cared for in their own homes, offering on-going support for, not only the patient, but also for their carers.

The recommendations in the Griffiths' Report places tremendous responsibility on the Social Services Departments and they will need to develop care plans for social/

health care and to appoint Care Managers who will be responsible in ensuring the agreed care plans are executed.

Care plans will need to be devised in consultation with members of the Primary Care Team, hospital and community services. Care plans will essentially concern all priority groups:

- elderly
- confused elderly
- people with learning difficulties
- mentally ill
- physically disabled
- children with special needs

The Primary Care Team needs to communicate with the Care Manager responsible for individual clients to ensure that the appropriate provision is made for clients' needs.

Each District has numerous voluntary organisations, some of which specialise in specific conditions, others are generic. Most Districts co-ordinate their voluntary services through a central organisation whose services are available to patients by self referral or any member of the Primary Health Care Team.

Apart from national groups there are local self help groups which provide services to patients with whom the Primary Care Team should be in contact.

All these groups and organisations can be identified via the local Council of Voluntary Services.

General Practitioner / Family Practitioner Committee

1991 and beyond will see an expanding role for FPCs which are due to develop into Family Health Services Authorities and their future role is currently being planned. It is probable that they will be included in the commissioning of health services for the district resident population.

The structure of FHSAs will be identical to that of future District Health Authorities in that there will be :

- five executive members
- five lay members
- chairperson appointed by the Secretary of State

There will be one medical executive member, which is a dramatic change from the current representation on FPCs, from general practice, dental practice, pharmacists and opticians.

The GP will continue to be responsible to the FHSAs which are under the direction of a General Manager who is responsible for the efficient and effective delivery of primary care services to the resident population. It will be the function of the General Manager to implement the GP Contract and to ensure that the highest standards of care are achieved in each District.

Medical advice to the General Manager will be achieved by the appointment of a Medical Officer for each FHSA.

It is essential that the voices of GPs and other professional groups, who are responsible for the day-to-day provision of health care, are heard by the authorities responsible for that care.

General Practitioner / Local Medical Committee

The members of the Local Medical Committees are elected to represent their colleagues in general practice and to liaise directly with all statutory and voluntary organisations which are responsible for the provision of health care.

The Local Medical Committee's prime interest is to ensure that a high standard of health care is provided to the resident population of the district. It is also to protect the interests of GPs and their patients and to ensure that the views of the Primary Care Team are addressed by all the providers of health and social care at all levels.

The LMC must now take on an expanding role, as identified in recent Departmental documents, and should include closer working relationships with:

- hospitals
- FPCs
- Social Services
- all organisations involved in provision of health and social care

Chapter 6

Records, Data and Information

The major effect of the New Contract is that particular attention has to be given to collection of data and providing information which has to be used for specific purposes. This has to start now and cannot wait for non-computerised practices to become computerised and for computerised practices to install new software.

There are a number of activities which have to be carried out that require keeping of records now! In this chapter we deal more with general principles than to dictate which method or system should be used. The final decisions have to be taken by each individual practice.

Questions to be Answered

Before deciding, attention must be given to the following questions:

- Why does data have to be collected ?
- What data and information has to be collected, for what purpose and for whom ?
- What records should be kept ?
- What system and what methods should be used ?
- Who should enter, keep and store the records?
- How, where and when should the records be kept ?

- What to do with the records ?
    - a) How to analyse
    - b) How to assess and evaluate findings
    - c) How to apply these to provide a better service
- How to present the outcomes for patient, doctor and NHS and to achieve changes and improvements ?

Why the need for comprehensive records?

The immediate reasons for better record keeping and actions are the requirements of the New Contract. It is most important for the practice to know more clearly what is going on and to have the facts on which to act. This is the first principle of good practice management. However, before embarking on data collection it is necessary to be clear on objectives. The requirements of the New Contract are clear - viz. targets to be met so that numerators (e.g. for cervical cytology and immunisation) have to be collected and also an accurate denominator (the group at risk, i.e. children requiring immunisation and women 26 - 65 in England & Wales and 20 - 60 in Scotland requiring cervical smears).

If the Practice is embarking on comprehensive record keeping then it should also consider collecting data on the work being done by all members of the team. Who was the work done for, how much work was done and where was it done ?

Efforts must be made to assess whether the available resources are being used effectively and efficiently in collating the records.

Finally the partners have to decide whether or not there is value for money in relation to the time being spent in collecting the records.

What data, on what, for whom?

The headings should include information on :

- the Practice
- the Patients
- the work being done
- housekeeping

All this should be put to an "audit" for consideration of the data, the outcomes, the implications and what changes, if any, need to be made.

The Practice

The immediate reason for setting out a profile of the Practice is that it will be available for the preparation of an Annual Report which each practice has to produce for the FPC.

Contents should include:

- the area of the Practice
- the premises available and how they are used
- the staff by names and roles
- the services provided, when, where and by whom
- general information and guidance

The Patients

It is now important to have accurate information on numbers of patients registered who actually "exist" and to eliminate inflation by virtue of those who are dead or have moved. An age/sex register must be available and be periodically checked with FPC data because, as well as "inflated patients", there will be some whom the FPC have not registered.

In addition to numbers it is necessary to check present addresses and telephone numbers. It is also helpful to record the occupations of patients and any special comments on family matters.

The Work

This is not a requirement for NHS purposes but will add greatly to interest in our activities and assist in making improvements.

The topics on which data is useful are:

- the amount of work actually done and analysed for:
  a) the Practice as a whole
  b) each GP
  c) each patient

- where the work is done i.e. office consultation, home visit or elsewhere

- what the work was done for ? Note the reason and, if possible, a diagnostic label

- what work was was actually done:
  was a prescription issued?
  was there a hospital referral ? If so - to which department in which hospital ?
  why was the referral made ?
  was it for X-ray or pathology etc ?
  was any special service such as cervical cytology or immunisation given ?

Such recordings should be carried out by the Practice Nurse as well as the GP.

- the result of the work ?

  It should be possible, but not easy, to get information on the outcome for the patient with regards to benefit or non benefit. Such information would be useful as well as interesting.

Housekeeping

The Practice Manager should have a data system on:

- staff
- pay-roll
- accounting
- stock control

"AUDIT"

To repeat collection of data is a useless exercise unless the data is put to some practical purpose in order to achieve changes for the better.

What records ?

Until there is a comprehensive computerised, all embracing, recording system for general practice, records have to be collected piece-meal for specific purposes. For each situation, and before any recording is contemplated, the whole exercise has to be worthwhile and the systems and methods feasible within the context of normal general practice. The work should not require more than a few seconds of consultation time with the entries being distinctive, accurate, valid and reproducable. It should, of course be useful for the practice.

Already there is a wealth of material and cards available for record keeping but the Practice has to be confident that, whatever it chooses, it can cope with.

- The FPC sends out regular computer printouts of practice lists, women due for cervical cytology and mammography and of children due for immunisation. These have to be checked by members of the Practice Team for accuracy and action.

- PACT send out quarterly data on personal and practice prescribing. A more detailed breakdown will be sent on request.

  The main problem here is that it takes up a lot of time to go through the sheets and there are few incentives to take any actions. The presentation should be made clearer, easier to follow and include "commentaries" on individual and practice prescribing patterns.

- There are many different sources of prepared record cards for general practice. These include RCGP, pharmaceutical companies and commercial printing firms whose names can be obtained from the RCGP.

- Computer software is available but at present it lacks uniformity and comprehensiveness.

"Me? A doctor? No! I just recycle FPC computer printouts."

Case Example - John Fry

For some 40 years a simple and useful system of recording has been in use in this S.E. London Practice of 8,500 patients. It started long before computerisation and has been entirely manual.

It has provided much material for analysis, application, research and reporting.

It consists of :

- Age-sex registers.
  One is based on FPC printouts transferred into a card index. The other has been used for over 30 years and consists of a log book divided into sections of 5 year dates of birth, e.g. 1950 - 1955, 1975 - 1980 and so on, with entries in alphabetical order. There are separate books for male and female. Also recorded is the date on which the patients first registered and if and when they left the practice.

- Work day sheets
  A separate page is used for each working day and entries are made for each consultation and home visit. The entry consists of name, sex, age group (in 5 year periods), diagnostic category (agreed into 20 system group and can be based on ICD) and whether a person is referred for X-ray (XR) or pathology (P) investigations or referred to hospital (H)

For example

GREEN M 5 - RESP - XR
BROWN F 65 - CVS - H

Each week these are entered into a prepared ledger-book with entries for numbers in various groups.
It is therefore possible to have up to date information on all

patient-doctor contacts divided into age, sex, diagnostic group and whether referred for XR, P or H.

From this data annual consultations per person can be calculated based on practice list size and related to other factors. It provides good material for annual reports.

- Clinical notes are the mainstay of all recording, whether manual or computerised. Attention must be paid to keep them legible and clear. It is useful to highlight important events and diagnoses and to have agreed ways of prescribing, making referrals and recording results of investigations.

- NHS summary cards and NHS immunisation cards should be used and completed.

- Special cards can also be used for obstetrics (RCGP card or NHS operation card) or those designed for child surveillance, well person and over 75s. However, extra cards increase bulk and take up space in filing cabinets.

- Cards may be used for repeat prescriptions but entry should also be made in the clinical notes.

- A Disease Index or Register should be created. The simple way of doing it is to have a notebook in your desk drawer which has separate sections for specific diseases. When a new diagnosis is made the person's name is entered with other brief identification details. Then, at leisure, names are transferred into a card index box for specific conditions. Therefore, with names related to disease it is possible to observe and analyse progress, outcome and natural history over the years occurring in a practice. The Disease Register is also useful for purposes of call and re-call of at-risk groups.

- Special records will be required for Health Promotion sessions and for running practice clinics for diabetes, asthma, obesity, anti smoking, heart disease, high blood pressure etc.

Information Technology: the Computer

Practice information is essential for efficient organisation as well as for monitoring and planning services to patients. Practice computer systems have only been developed in recent years and are currently undergoing radical development to cater for the needs of a busy practice. The Department of Health is currently writing software for the implementation of indicative prescribing and for budget holding.

Information requirements for monitoring patient activity and completion of annual reports are best achieved through a computer system and software provision is made to audit the information to complete these programmes.

Practice computers can be used for :

- age/sex register
- disease register
- prescribing records
- repeat prescriptions
- monitoring prescribing
- call and re-call systems
- word processing
- audit
- Practice finances
- payrolls
- networking with Hospital and FPC

Information is refined data and the information generated by a computer is as reliable as the data that is entered into the system. A high level of accuracy of input is essential.

Establishing a computer system

The initial content of the Practice List can be obtained from the FPC which has to be checked against the records held within the Practice to ensure the accuracy of the download.

All patients records should be analysed and the following should be recorded:

- registration details including post code & 'phone numbers
- important clinical conditions to form a disease index
- medication (current)
- completed screening programmes
- immunisation status
- recall markers

Markers

Markers are an essential component of general practice computer systems and each practice is free to use available markers to identify any practice activity.

It is a simple matter to call up any activity by locating the appropriate marker, e.g. using markers to complete the New Contract:

- identifying 75-year olds as they are screened
- completing child surveillance
- new entrants on joining list
- new entrants having completed their screening programme which gives the information for those to whom invitations should be extended to attend the Practice for screening
- consultation marker
- clinical recall

Data Collection

The Practice needs to devise a system whereby all activity is fed into the computer. This must start with patient registration, their screening data included in the previous sub-headings and all clinical data undertaken by the primary care team. This includes:

- consultations
- diagnoses
- investigations
- medication
- review
- hospital referrals

Nevertheless, manual records need to be retained for recording such information as treatment programmes and detailed hospital reports.

Access to Information

All computer systems have to be registered under the Data Protection Act. This entry is regularly reviewed and any changes of detail have to be identified.

Access to Information Act allows patients to access any information recorded on the computer on payment of a minimal fee to the practice.

What to do with Data

It is no use collecting data unless practical use is made of it to improve services and to educate and stimulate the Practice team. Therefore, someone or some small working party in the practice must look at and analyse the data and present it in understandable form to practice colleagues for discussion and action.

Chapter 7

Managing the Practice and the Team

To operate the new GP Contract effectively it is essential for any practice to be well organised. Effective organisation is a complex matter and will depend on the cohesiveness and strength of the primary care team.

The Primary Care Team consists of:

- General Practitioner(s)
- Practice Manager
- Practice Nurse(s)
- Reception Staff
- Secretary(s)
- Clerical Staff
- Computer Input Clerks

Attached Staff include:

- District Nurse(s)
- Health Visitor
- District Midwife/Midwives
- Community Psychiatric Nurses

Associated Members of the Team:

- Social Worker
- Community Rehabilitation services including Physiotherapy and Occupational Therapy

Influences on Practice Activity

The staff employed by the Practice, and their organisation, will depend on the activity that the Practice wishes to undertake albeit that all services are not mandatory. These include and depend on:

- general medical services
- GP Contract
- patient needs
- facilities within the Practice
- staff employed

General Practice provides a general medical primary care service. General Practitioners and their staff's first priority remains that of treating their patients health needs and maintaining a high quality of care. Patients' growing expectations continue to put an increased demand on primary care.

Organisation

To provide the full spectrum of care that is now expected in general practice, practice survival will depend on reliable organisation which can only be achieved by effective management. The organisation of the Practice will be governed by the following factors :

- day to day management - administrative and clinical
- roles of team members
- inter-relationships between members
- communication
- quality
- audit
- accommodation available

Clinical Management

Clinical management is the responsibility of the GP who should decide the details of clinical care that will be provided by the Practice using the Statement of Fees and Allowances ("The Red Book") guidelines.

- hours of availability to patients for general medical services and specialist clinics required by the new GP contract
- agreed daily work programme
- access to the doctor by the patient, either personalised lists or open access
- provision of home visits
- out of hours cover through rota arrangements with local colleagues or deputising services
- mechanisms for home assessments
- establishment of protocols and completion of practice formulary
- close liaison with practice nurses

The role and functions of the practice nurse have to be agreed and any extension of roles requires further education, training and assessment with a Certificate of Competence and working within agreed written and signed practice protocols.

Management / Administration: Practice Manager

Management is best achieved by the employment of a practice manager who is responsible for the day to day organisation and the efficient running of the Practice.

The administrative staff responsible to the Manager include:

- receptionists
- secretaries
- clerks
- data input personnel
- financial clerk
- telephonist
- appointments clerk

As well as the supervision of the staff the Practice Manager has other responsibilities to include:

- maintenance of the property
- cleaning
- holiday cover
- stock control
- replenishing stocks
- equipment maintenance
- duty rosters
- holiday/sickness cover
- contracts of employment including job descriptions
- performance review(s)
- in-house education programmes

It is part of the function of the Practice Manager to identify the roles of administrative staff in the Practice and ensure that a close working relationship is maintained between administrative and clinical members of the team. It is essential that clearly identified functions are allocated to each member of the staff. All staff should be aware of each other's function.

The Practice Manager should also co-ordinate the holiday arrangements for all members of the primary care team so that holiday overlap is avoided and suitable cover is arranged.

The Practice Manager should liaise closely with the professional managers of statutory authorities and voluntary agencies including District Nurses, Health Visitors, Community Psychiatric Nurses and Social Workers.

The developments in general practice beyond the Contract will require increasing co-operation with community personnel employed by District Health Authorities and primary care team members working in general practice. This development must extend to our Local Authority colleagues when Care Managers are established, in keeping with the "Care in the Community" document.

Communication

Communication is an essential feature of good management and strenuous efforts must be made within the Practice to develop good communication links between patients and all members of staff. This can be achieved through :

- practice leaflet
- practice notice board
- suggestion box
- practice interest(s) groups
- practice newsletter
- regular practice staff meetings
- practice clinical meetings

Quality

We should be continually aware of the service we provide in general practice to ensure that the care provided is of a high level. Measurements of the quality of care can, in some aspects, be made by :

- provision of facilities
- efficiency of appointment times
- length of waiting time to be seen
- operating flexible systems within the Practice to suit patient's needs
- undertaking regular staff performance review
- efficiency of communications
- operating standards within agreed protocols

Audit and Clinical Reviews

"Audit" is a continual process which should be undertaken as part of the organisation of the Practice and we should continually review the service provision to patients in the spectrum and the extension of the care provided. It should be a simple non threatening exercise to staff and should not become exaggerated or complex. The main purposes are to check on measures and protocols previously agreed to define problems and then to try and correct them.

Clinical reviews should be undertaken on a regular basis between all the clinical members of the team so as to ensure that an efficient but meaningful service is provided to patients. Clinical cases should be presented and discussed, outcomes examined and adjustments made where appropriate to ensure the highest possible level of care.

The developments in General Practice in recent years have necessitated increasing requirements for space to accommodate new staff, provide a fuller spectrum of care and to fit in new equipment and machinery. The New Contract has compounded this requirement and to some extent the space available in the Practice may govern the activities which a practice can undertake.

In addition to traditional facilities of consulting rooms, waiting space, office and meeting rooms, attention must be given to :

- accommodation for health promotion clinic(s) for at least 10 participants
- accommodation for computer(s) and input clerks
- accommodation for attached staff
- treatment room facilities